Real Science-4-Kids

# Biology

# Level I
## Laboratory Workbook

Dr. R. W. Keller

RealScience 4 Kids

*Cover design*: David Keller
*Opening page*: David Keller, Rebecca Keller
*Illustrations*:  Rebecca Keller

**Copyright © 2004, 2007  Gravitas Publications, Inc.**

Real Science-4-Kids:  Biology Level I- Laboratory Workbook

**ISBN 0-9749149-3-2**

Published by Gravitas Publications, Inc.
P.O. Box 4790
Albuquerque, NM 87196-4790

GRAVITAS
PUBLICATIONS INC

# Keeping a Laboratory Notebook

A laboratory notebook is essential for the experimental scientist.  In this notebook, the results for all of the experiments are kept together with comments and any additional information.  For this curriculum, you should record your experimental observations and conclusions directly on these pages, which are designated as the laboratory notebook, just like real scientists.

The experimental section for each chapter is pre written.  The exact format of a notebook may vary among scientists, but all experiments written in a laboratory notebook have certain essential parts.  For each experiment, a descriptive but short *Title* is written at the top of the page along with the *Date* the experiment is performed.   Below the title, an *Objective* and *Hypothesis* are written.  The objective is a short statement that tells something about why you are doing the experiment, and the hypothesis is the predicted outcome.  Next, a *Materials List* is written. The materials should be gathered before the experiment is started.  Following the materials list, the *Experiment* is written.  The sequence of steps for the experiment is written beforehand, and any changes should be noted during the experiment.  All of the details of the experiment are written in this section. All information that might be of some importance is included.  For example, if you are to measure out 1 cup of water for an experiment, but you actually measured 1 1/4 cup, this should be recorded.  It is hard sometimes to predict how small variations in an experiment will affect the outcome and it is easier to track a problem if all of the information is recorded.

The next section is the *Results* section.  Here you will record your experimental observations.  It is extremely important that you be honest about what is observed.  For example if the experimental instructions say that a solution will turn yellow, but your solution turned blue -- record blue.  You may have done the experiment incorrectly or you might have discovered a new and interesting result, but either way it is very important that your observations be honestly recorded.

Finally, the *Conclusions* should be written.  Here you will explain what the observations may mean.  You should try to write only *valid* conclusions.  It is important to learn to think about what the data actually show and what cannot be concluded from the experiment.

# Laboratory Safety

Most of these experiments use household items. Extra care should be taken while working with all chemicals in this series of experiments. The following are some general laboratory precautions that should be applied to the home laboratory:

Never put things in your mouth without explicit instructions to do so. This means that food items should not be eaten unless tasting or eating is part of the experiment.

If glasses are not available, kids/teachers should get them. Use safety glasses while using glass objects or strong chemicals such as bleach.

Wash hands before and after handling chemicals.

Use adult supervision while working with sharp objects and while conducting any step requiring a stove.

# Contents

Experiment 1:     Putting things in order          Date: _____

Objective:  In this experiment we will try to organize a variety of objects into categories

Materials:

Collect a variety of objects.  Some suggested items are rubber balls, oranges, cotton balls, banana, apple, paper, sticks, leaves, and grass.

Experiment:

1.  Spread all of the objects on a table.  Carefully look at each object and note some of irs characteristics.  For example, some objects will be round or fuzzy; some will be edible, others not; some may be large, some small; and so on.

2.  Record your observations for each item in the Results section.

3.  Try to define "categories" for the objects.  For example, some objects may be "hard," so one category can be called "Hard." Some objects may be "round," so another category can be "Round."  Try to think of at least 4 or 5 different categories for your objects.  Write the categories along the top of the graph in the Results section.

4.  List the objects that fit into these categories.  Note those objects that can fit into more than one category. Write these objects down more than once, if necessary, under all of the categories they fit.

5.  Take a look at each of the categories and each of the objects in those categories.  Can you make "sub-categories"? For example, some objects may all have the same color, so "Red" can be a sub-category, or some may be food items so "Food" can be a subcategory.  Try to list several sub-categories for each of the categories.

6. List the objects according to their category and subcategory.

## Results:

| Item | Characteristics |
| --- | --- |
|  |  |
|  |  |
|  |  |
|  |  |
|  |  |
|  |  |
|  |  |
|  |  |
|  |  |
|  |  |
|  |  |

| Categories | | | | | | |
|---|---|---|---|---|---|---|
|  |  |  |  |  |  |  |
|  |  |  |  |  |  |  |

| | | | | | | Categories |
|---|---|---|---|---|---|---|
| | | | | | | Subcategories |
|  |  |  |  |  |  |  |

Conclusions:

_____

_____

_____

_____

_____

_____

_____

_____

_____

● Review

What is taxonomy?   _____

_____

List the five kingdoms   _____      _____

_____      _____

_____

List the other six categories for classifying living things

_____      _____

_____      _____

_____      _____

● Which kingdom are dogs, cats, and frogs in?   _____

Which phylum are dogs, cats, and frogs in?   _____

Which  class  are  frogs  _____  in?

Which  order  are  dogs  _____  in?

Which  family  are  cats  _____  in?

What is the Latin name given to humans and what does it mean?

_____

●

Experiment 2:          Inside the cell          Date: _____

Look at the drawings of the three types of cells from the text.  Observe the similarities and the differences for the three types of cells.

Write down some observations of things that are similar for all cell types:

_____

_____

_____

Write down some observations of things that are different:

_____

_____

_____

Write down the function for each of the following:

<u>Nucleus</u> _____

<u>Mitochondria</u> _____

<u>Chloroplast</u> _____

<u>Cell wall</u> _____

<u>Lysosome</u> _____

<u>Peroxisome</u> _____

● How do animal cells differ from plant cells, and how do both plant and animal cells differ from bacterial cells?

List as many reasons as you can for the differences among bacteria, plants, and animals. Tell why you think their cells may differ.

| Bacteria (have or don't have...) | Plants (have or don't have...) | Animals (have or don't have...) |
|---|---|---|
|  |  |  |
|  |  |  |
|  |  |  |
|  |  |  |
|  |  |  |
|  |  |  |
|  |  |  |
|  |  |  |
|  |  |  |
|  |  |  |

Without looking at your text, fill in the blanks with as many names for the structures in the cell as you can.  Color the cell.

Is this an animal cell, a plant cell, or a prokaryotic cell?  Write the cell type at the top.

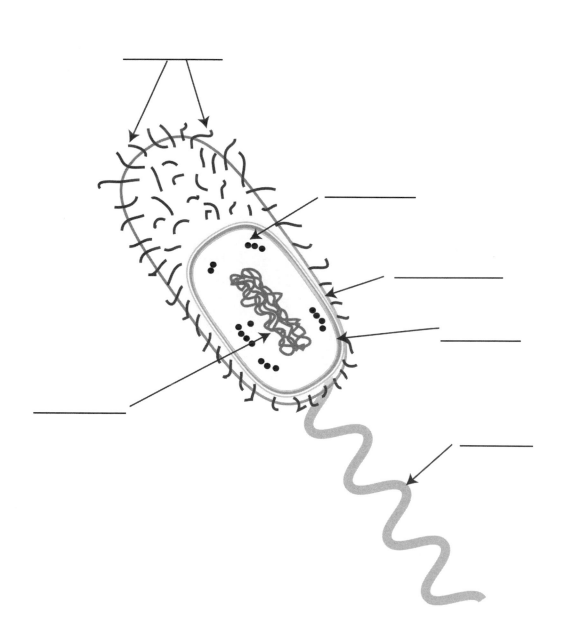

●Without looking at your text, try to fill in the names of as many of the structures as
you can.

Is this an animal cell, a plant cell, or a prokaryotic cell?  Write the type
of cell at the top.

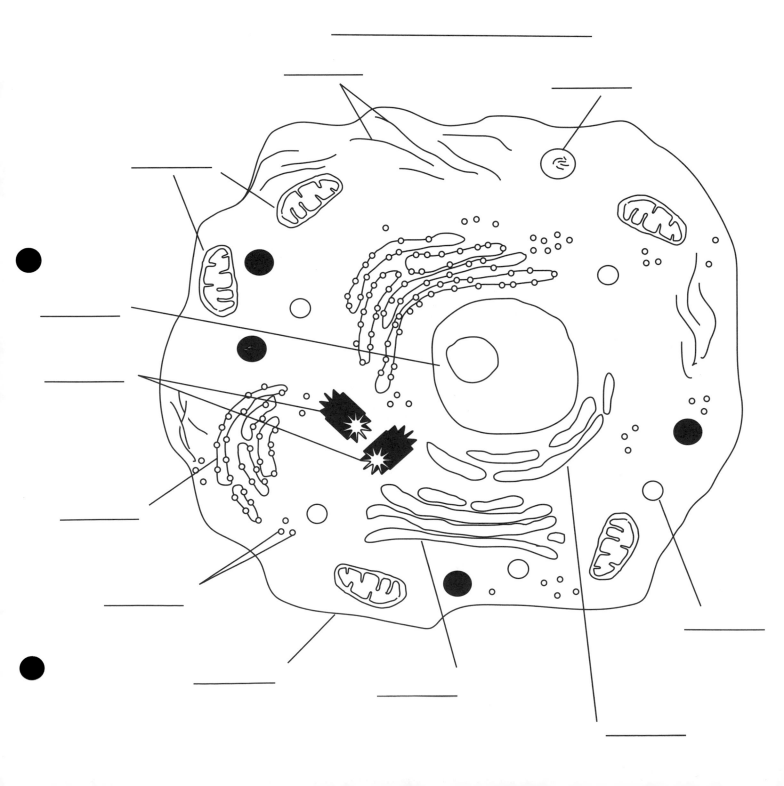

Without looking at your text, fill in the blanks with the names for as many of the structures in the cell as you can.  Color the cell.

Is this an animal cell, a plant cell, or a prokaryotic cell?  Write the type of cell at the top.

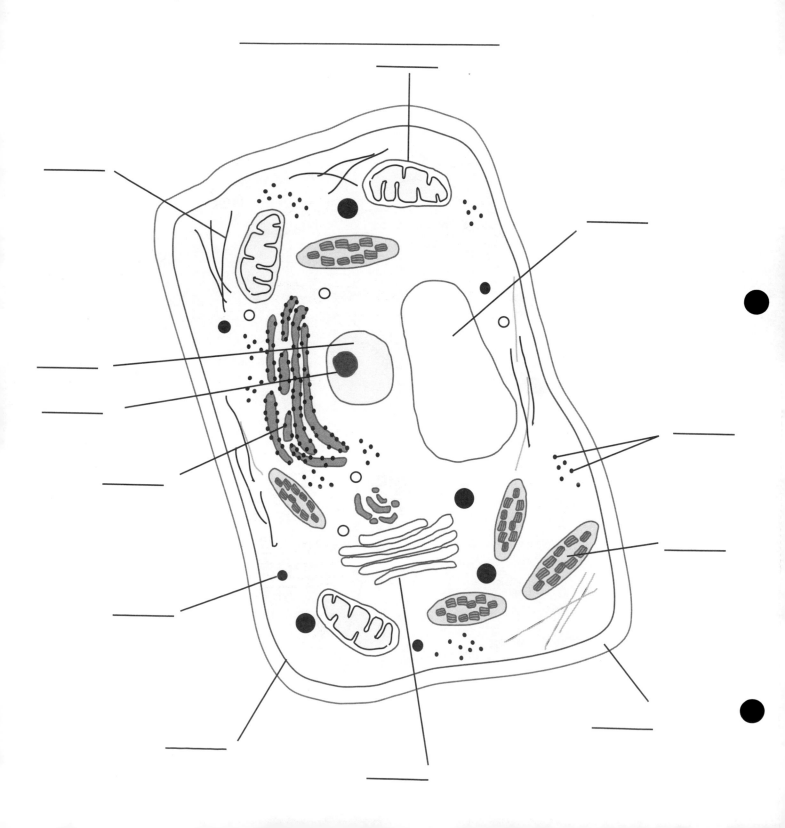

Conclusions:

Review

Answer the following questions:

What are cells made of?    _____

What are tissues made of?    _____

What are organs made of?    _____

Define the following terms:

prokaryote    _____

eukaryote    _____

organelle    _____

Name some organelles found in plant and animal cells:

_____        _____

_____        _____

_____        _____

What does a flagellum do?    _____

Where are chloroplasts mostly found? _____

What are mitochondria for? _____

# NOTES:

Experiment 3:     Take away the light          Date:_____

Objective:    _____

_____

_____

_____

_____

Hypothesis:    _____

_____

_____

Materials:

    lightweight cardboard or construction paper
    tape
    plant with flat leaves (6)
    small jars
    marker

Experiment:

1. Take some cardboard or construction paper and cut it into squares large enough to cover the front and back of a leaf.

2. We will test six different leaves.  Two of the leaves will be left on the plant (attached) and four leaves will be removed from the plant (unattached).

3. One attached leaf will be covered and one attached leaf will be uncovered. One of the four unattached leaves will be covered in water, one uncovered in water, one uncovered out of water, and one covered out of water.

4. With the marker, label the leaves in the following manner:
        Leaf 1:  UA- uncovered, attached
        Leaf 2: CA- covered, attached
        Leaf 3: UUW- uncovered, unattached, in water
        Leaf 4: CUW- covered, unattached, in water
        Leaf 5: UU- uncovered, unattached (no water)
        Leaf 6: CU- covered, unattached (no water)

5. Take two small jars and fill them with water.  Take the two leaves that will be placed in the water and prop them in the jars keeping the stems submerged.  Check the water level every day over the course of the experiment to make sure there is enough water in the jars.

6. Observe the changes to the leaves daily by carefully removing the cardboard and then retaping it. Record your observations.

Results:

Observations:

|        | UA | CA | UUW | CUW | UU | CU |
|--------|----|----|-----|-----|----|----|
| Day 1  |    |    |     |     |    |    |
| Day 2  |    |    |     |     |    |    |
| Day 3  |    |    |     |     |    |    |
| Day 4  |    |    |     |     |    |    |
| Day 5  |    |    |     |     |    |    |
| Day 6  |    |    |     |     |    |    |
| Day 7  |    |    |     |     |    |    |
| Day 8  |    |    |     |     |    |    |
| Day 9  |    |    |     |     |    |    |
| Day 10 |    |    |     |     |    |    |

Conclusions:

_____

_____

_____

_____

_____

_____

_____

_____

_____

_____

_____

_____

_____

_____

_____

_____

# Review

● Define the following terms:

photosynthesis _____

_____

chloroplast _____

_____

chlorophyll _____

_____

● conifer _____

_____

algae _____

_____

cyanobacteria _____

_____

How do most green plants get their food?  Do they eat cheeseburgers?

_____

_____

●

Experiment 4:      Colorful flowers         Date: _____

Objective: _____
_____

Hypothesis: _____
_____
_____
_____

Materials:

small jars
2 or more white carnation flowers
food coloring

Experiment:

1.  Put water in several small jars and add several drops of food coloring.

2.  Trim the ends of one carnation stem and place it in the colored water.

3.  Watch the petals of the carnation and record any color changes observed.

4.  Take out the carnation and cut a small slice of the stem off from the bottom. Try to identify the xylem and the phloem.  Draw a picture of what you see in the Results section.  Cut the carnation flower lengthwise.  Try to identify the parts of the flower.

5.  Take one stem and slice it about halfway towards the flower lengthwise with a knife. (Have an adult help you.)  Stick one end in a solution of colored water and place the other end in a different color of water.  Let the carnation soak up the colored water until the petals begin to change color.  Draw a picture of what you observe in the Results section.

Results:

## Conclusions:

_____

_____

_____

_____

_____

_____

_____

_____

_____

_____

_____

## Review

Define the following terms:

1. xylem  _____

2. phloem  _____

3. pith  _____

4. pollen  _____

5. stamen  _____

6. ovary  _____

Name the four main parts of a plant:

1. _____

2. _____

3. _____

4. _____

Name two types of roots:

1. _____

2. _____

Experiment 5:        Which way is down?              Date: _____

Objective:    _____

_____

Hypothesis:    _____

_____

Materials:

    small jars (2)
    several pinto beans
    absorbent white paper
    plastic wrap
    clear tape
    two rubber bands

Experiment:

1.  Cut strips of white paper the width of the jars.

2. Label each strip "A", "B", "C", and "D" with a few centimeters between each
   letter.

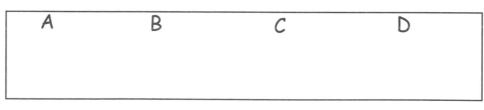

3.  Place the beans in different directions on the labels with clear tape.

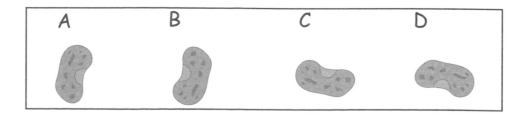

4. Place the paper with the attached beans gently inside the small jar. The beans should be between the jar and the paper.

5. Place one or two more beans in between the jar and paper, but don't tape these. These beans will be opened and examined before the roots completely emerge

6. Add some water to the bottom of the jar, but don't submerge the beans.

7. Cover the jar with plastic wrap and secure it with a rubber band. Place the jar in direct sunlight.

8. With the second jar, repeat steps 1-7, but place the jar in a dark room.

9. In a few days the beans will start to grow. When the beans begin to change, take out one of the loose beans and gently cut it open. [Have an adult help.] Try to identify the different parts of the embryo.

10. Continue to observe the growth of the beans. Watch and record their change every few days. Try to determine if the beans placed in different directions grow differently. Compare the beans grown in the light with those grown in the dark.

Results:        Draw the parts of the embryo here:

DAY ___                     LIGHT

| A | B | C | D |
| --- | --- | --- | --- |
|   |   |   |   |

DAY ___

| A | B | C | D |
| --- | --- | --- | --- |
|   |   |   |   |

DAY ___

| A | B | C | D |
| --- | --- | --- | --- |
|   |   |   |   |

DAY ___

| A | B | C | D |
| --- | --- | --- | --- |
|   |   |   |   |

DAY ____                    DARK

| A | B | C | D |
|---|---|---|---|
|   |   |   |   |

DAY ____

| A | B | C | D |
|---|---|---|---|
|   |   |   |   |

DAY ____

| A | B | C | D |
|---|---|---|---|
|   |   |   |   |

DAY ____

| A | B | C | D |
|---|---|---|---|
|   |   |   |   |

Record your observations for each bean on the previous pages.  It may take several days to see a change.  Record the day that you observe a change.  Draw a picture of each bean on the days you observe a change.

Conclusions:

_____

_____

_____

_____

_____

_____

_____

_____

_____

_____

_____

_____

_____

_____

Review
● Define the following terms

seed _____

seedling _____

seed coat _____

cotyledon _____

embryo _____

germination _____

● Name two plant signals

1. _____

2. _____

List the four stages in the life cycle of a flowering plant

1. _____

2. _____

3. _____

4. _____

●

Experiment 6:        How do they move?        Date: _____ ●

Objective: _____
_____

Hypothesis: _____
_____

Materials:

microscope
microscope slides (WARD'S Glass Depression Slides, 14-D-3510)
eye droppers (3)
fresh pond water or water mixed with soil
Protozoa study kit (WARD'S Protist Set 1, 87-D-1530)

Experiment: ●

1. Familiarize yourself with your microscope before beginning this lesson. Read the instruction manual for your microscope, if it is available, and try to look at any prepared samples that may have come with your microscope. If you already know how to operate a microscope, skip this step.

2. Take one of the protozoa samples and place a small droplet onto a glass slide that has been correctly positioned in the microscope.

3. Observe the movement of protozoa. If the organisms move too quickly, apply a droplet of Protoslo to the glass slide.

4. Patiently observe the movement of the protozoa. Note the type of protozoa in the Results section. Try to describe how the protozoa moves. Write down as many observations as you can.

5. Repeat step 4 with the other two protozoan types. ●

6. Now take a droplet of fresh pond water and place it on a slide to veiw under the microscope. Try to determine the types of protozoa you observe based on how the organism moves. Write your results in the Results section.

## Results:

Name _____

Describe movement:

Name _____

Describe movement:

Name _____

Describe movement:

Draw what you observed in the pond water.

Conclusions:

Review

Define the following terms:

protist_____

microscope_____

cilia _____

flagellum _____

pseudopod _____

Draw a paramecium.

Draw a euglena.

Draw an amoeba

How do euglena and paramecia move? _____

_____

How does an amoeba move? _____

# NOTES:

Experiment 7:          How do they eat?          Date: _____

Objective: _____

_____

Hypothesis: _____

_____

Materials:

Protozoa study kit (from Experiment 6)
Congo Red stain (WARD'S Natrual Science, 944 V 9504)
baker's yeast
distilled water
microscope
microscope slides
eye droppers (3)

## Making Cong-Red-stained yeast:

This step needs to be completed before continuing with the experiment.

- Add one teaspoon of dried yeast to ½ cup of distilled water.  Allow it to dissolve.
- Add one droplet of Congo Red dye to one droplet of yeast mixture. Observe the mixture under the microscope.  You should be able to observe the individual yeast cells stained red.

## Experiment:

1. Take either the paramecia or amoeba samples and place a small droplet onto a glass slide that has been correctly positioned in the microscope.

2. Take a small droplet of the Congo-Red-stained yeast and place it into the droplet of protozoa.

3. Patiently observe the protozoa and note the red-colored yeast.  Try to describe how the protozoa eats.  Write down as many observations as you can.

4. Repeat steps 2-4 with the other protozoa.

5. Record your observations below.

Results:

Draw a picture showing how amoebas eat.

Draw a picture showing how paramecia eat.

Conclusions:

_____

_____

_____

_____

_____

_____

_____

_____

_____

_____

_____

_____

_____

_____

_____

_____

# Review

Define the following terms:

stigma_____

food vacuole_____

phagocytosis_____

oral groove_____

cytoplasm_____


What is *Didinium*?      _____

What is *Podophyra*?     _____

# NOTES:

- _____
  _____
  _____
  _____
  _____
  _____
  _____
  _____
  _____
  _____

- _____
  _____
  _____
  _____
  _____
  _____
  _____
  _____
  _____
  _____

- _____
  _____

Experiment 8:          From tadpole to frog          Date:_____

Objective:    _____
              _____

Materials:

      tadpole
      tadpole food
      small aquarium
      tap water conditioner and tap water
      OR
      distilled water

## Experiment:

1. Use distilled water or "cure" 1 gallon tap water by adding tap water conditioner. "Curing" removes any harmful chemicals like chlorine that are found in tap water.

2. Fill the aquarium $\frac{1}{2}$ to $\frac{3}{4}$ full with the conditioned or distilled water.

3. Add the live tadpoles.

4. Feed the tadpoles according to the directions.

5. Observe the changes the tadpoles make over the course of 4 to 6 weeks.

6. Record your observations in the Results section.  See if you can identify the different stages of the tadpole outlined in this chapter. (Note when the legs emerge, the time it takes for the front legs to emerge, etc.)

Draw the various stages in the life cycle of frogs.

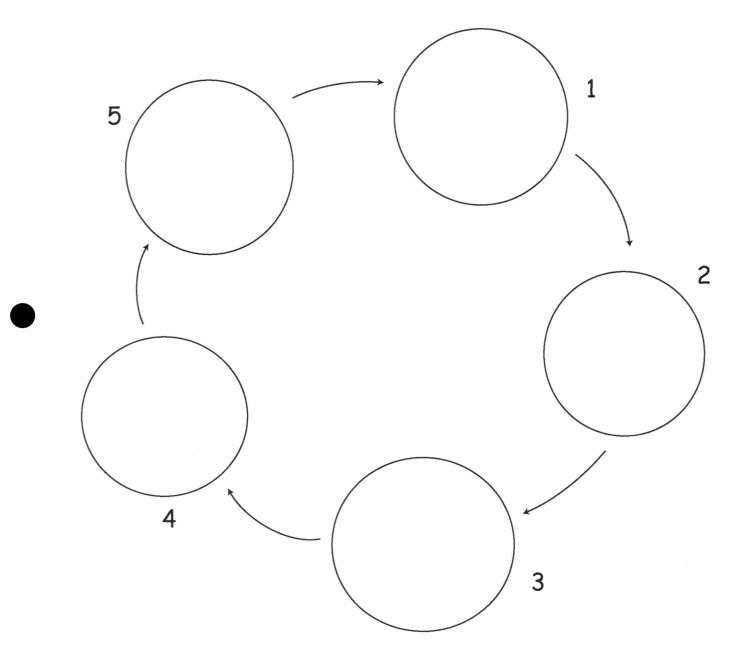

# Label the parts of the frog.

Results:

Week

1 _____

2 _____

3 _____

4 _____

5 _____

6 _____

7 _____

8 _____

9 _____

10 _____

11 _____

12 _____


Conclusions:

_____

_____

_____

_____

Reveiw

Define the following terms:

spawning _____

amphibian _____

metamorphosis _____

tympanic membrane _____

# NOTES:

Experiment 9 :        From caterpillar to butterfly        Date: _____

Objective:        _____

_____

Hypothesis:        _____

_____

Materials:

        caterpillar or butterfly kit
        small cage

Experiment:

1. Follow the directions on the butterfly kit for proper care of your caterpillar or provide food for your local caterpillar.

2. Fill out the life cycle chart on the page 47.

3. Over the course of the next several weeks, observe any changes your caterpillar undergoes.

4. Record how much food your caterpillar eats.

5 Record how many times the caterpillar molts.

6. Record where the caterpillar spins its cocoon.

7. If you can observe the caterpillar emerging, record how long before it can fly.

Draw the various stages in the life cycle of a butterfly,

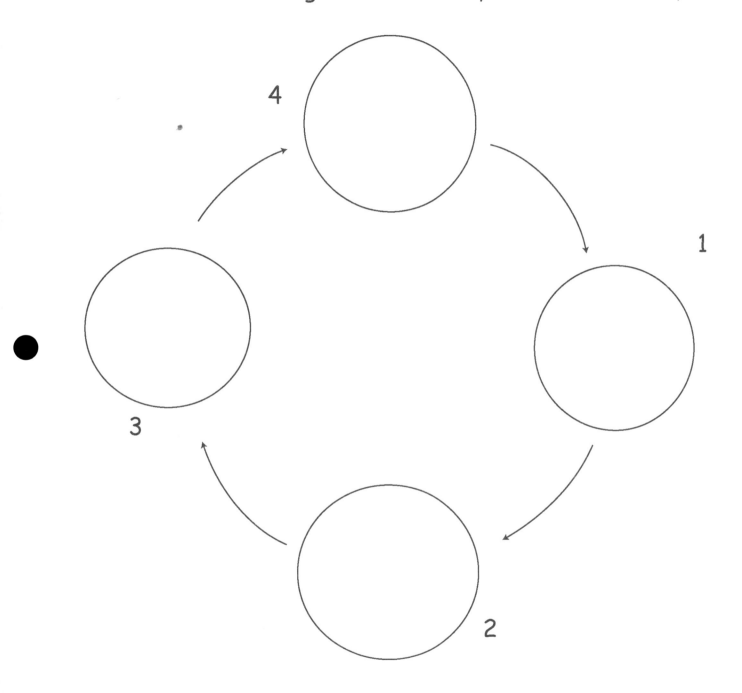

Results:

| Week | Amount of food eaten | Molting? | Other observations |
|------|----------------------|----------|--------------------|
| 1 | | | |
| 2 | | | |
| 3 | | | |
| 4 | | | |
| 5 | | | |
| 6 | | | |
| 7 | | | |
| 8 | | | |
| 9 | | | |
| 10 | | | |
| 11 | | | |
| 12 | | | |

Conclusions:

_____

_____

_____

_____

# Review

● Define the following terms:

lepidoptera
_____
_____

larval stage
_____
_____

molting
_____
_____

● 

pupal stage
_____
_____

chrysalis
_____
_____

imago
_____
_____

●

Experiment 10:         Making an ecosystem         Date: _____

Objective: _____

_____

Materials:

clear glass or plastic tank with a solid lid
small plants
soil
small bugs such as worms, ants, small beetles, etc.

Experiment:

1.  Take the glass or plastic container and cover the bottom with water.

2.  Place the lid on the container and allow it to sit overnight.

3.  Record your observations in Part I A of the Results section.

4.  Remove the lid and let it sit overnight again.

5.  Record your results in Part I B of the Results section.

6.  Place the soil on the bottom of the container.  Put in enough soil to fill the container about 1/3 full.

7.  Plant the small plants in the soil.

8.  Add the small bugs to the plants.

9.  Place the lid on the container and record in Part II any changes in your ecosystem over the next several weeks.

This is now a small ecosystem.

Results:

Part I A _____

Part I B _____

Part II

| | | |
|---|---|---|
| | | |
| | | |

Conclusions:

# Review

● Define the following terms:

ecosystem _____
_____

cycle _____
_____

food cycle _____
_____

●

air cycle _____
_____

water cycle _____
_____

NOTES:

NOTES:

# Extra Graphing Paper

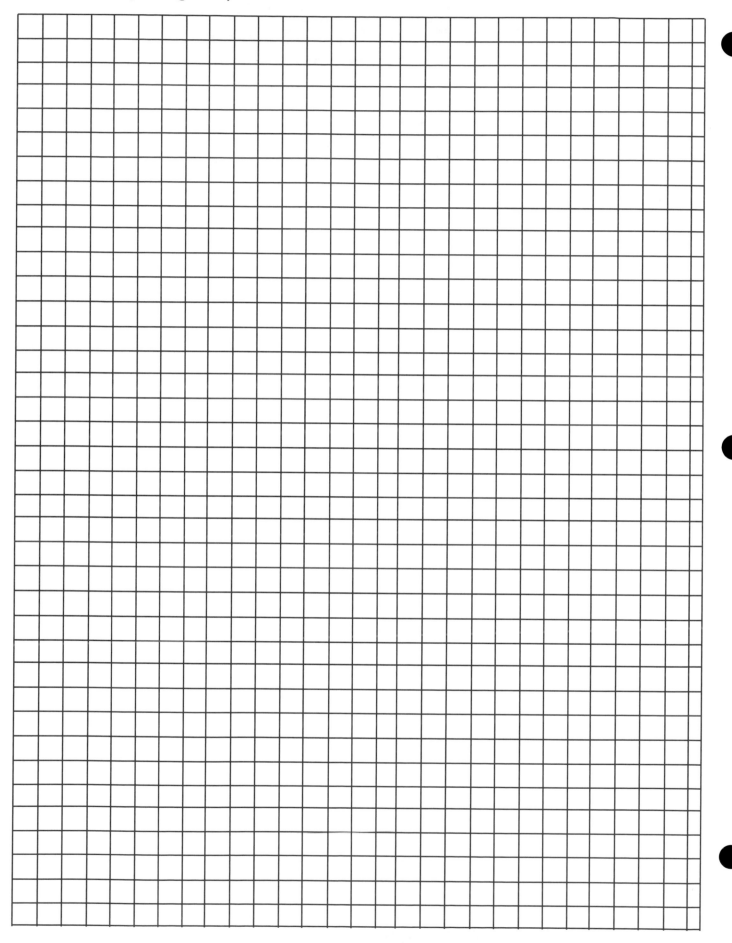

# Extra Graphing Paper